May the Words Holed up Inside me Find their Way to You

Shiyanne Stuart

BookLeaf
Publishing

Presentation by *BookLeaf Publishing*

Web: www.bookleafpub.com

E-mail: info@bookleafpub.com

ISBN: 9789358367997

First edition 2023

*To all those who said I could, but especially to
all those who said I couldn't*

ACKNOWLEDGEMENT

I would like to thank my Mom and Dad for telling me I could do anything I wanted. I would like to thank my brother for telling me the reality of life. I would like to thank my friends for telling me I should be a writer, and I would like to thank my roommate for helping me survive my freshman year of college. And lastly BookLeaf Publishing for this opportunity. This book is for all of you.

To Start Again

Forget the way you knew me, for that is not me

But don't forget who I was because it will
always be part of me

I am new

I am old

I am everything and I am nothing

I am a god amongst kings and a soul drifting in
the wind

When I am different, note that I am the same I
have always been

Only now, I am letting you in

Sugar-Coated Oxygen

Loving you gave me the air in my lungs, and
when you left I found I was gasping for your
sugar-coated oxygen

It sickens me you had this effect, but you were
always so direct

Your sweet nothings and promises of great
things were what gave me my faulty wings

And now I'm stuck on the ground, looking for
something more profound

But all I see is the memories you gave to me

To you

all the lines I wrote to you

seem to matter so little

when compared to the love I have for you

Crossing

Cross the road

but what will i find?

If you're lucky, the beauty on the other side

and if not?

Well, then at least you can say that you tried

Profound

I keep thinking I have to say something
profound

But I keep finding there's nothing profound for
me to say

Sometimes things are just words

And that's okay

That's okay

Funny poetry

Why can't poetry be funny?

Probably because most poets don't know how to
have fun

.

It's me, I don't know how to have fun

And Yet

It's foolish to think that something is going to be
easy just because you're good at it

The task is still difficult, you simply manage to
persist in spite of it

Moon

I always wondered why we look to the moon
and stars to guide us

But I think it's because they give us comfort in a
world that seems insistent on lying to us

When I look at the moon I find comfort in its
glow

And I know it's seen more of my starlight tears
than the rest of the world will ever know

The Body

The Skeleton is the wishes and the dreams

And the flesh is the hopes and the desires

The muscles are the emotions and the thoughts

But the soul is all that and more

The Mind

The soul shares the emotion of the brain and wit
shares the feelings of the soul

To be both witty and honest is to be at one with
your pain and walk with your head held high

Dead Roses

There's something about dead roses

And what they mean to me

How they express love and compassion until
they wilt away

There's something about dead roses

And what they say

How a wilted rose will mean something different
than the healthy one of yesterday

There's something about dead roses

And the connection of how love fades away

With how an eerie fragrance lingers despite the
gentle rot

There's something about dead roses

But I'm not sure what they say

Love is

When you are sick and you're determined not to make someone else bare the burden of it

So you fight and you kick knowing that the nausea of opening up is worse than just being sick

It works for a while and you pretend you'll get better if you just sleep it off

It's still better than making someone share the burden of you being sick

Your body aches and your head throbs, the cold chills are just your imagination, that's all

It's a stuffy nose you insist as someone gets past that imaginary 5-foot stick

You're weak and tired, you're hot and you're shaking, but this is *still* better than sharing the burden of being sick

But it's not

And you know that too

So when someone finally comes knocking with
the firm promise that they'll be alright

In a bleary-eyed haze such logic seems airtight

And it helps, and your body aches less, and the
nausea subsides

And when they get sniffles maybe that's okay

Maybe love is saying it's okay to ask for help
and not pretend to be fine

Maybe just maybe

Love is a stuffy nose

Believe

"I believe in you"

I'm so sick of those hollow words I know you
think are true

I'm glad you believe in me, but I don't believe
you

I'm not amazing or beautiful and smart

My words are not some masterpiece or work of
art

I'm only me, and that's all I'll ever be

In response you said to me:

My love has no such conditions or restraints

That you love me

Simply because I'm me

So maybe I can believe in those seemingly
hollow words

As long as "I love you" comes before "I believe
in you"

4 AM

In: the light of the day

Som: ething new will always show through

Ni: ggling, always and ever-present

A: nd as a new day dawns, so too will you

Errands

Go fetch errand boy.

Never let them see how utterly broken you are,
how the glass you walk on kills you quietly,

never assure them that you are fine.

Sidelong glances and whispers to the moon.
Always stay hidden.

Live for others, never yourself.

Go fetch errand boy, go fetch.

Consequences

I will always suffer the consequences of loving you

But let me make it clear

I will never regret coming to know you

Almost

But let's not spoil the end with the greedy wishes
of the now

Because all the best stories begin and end with
asking the question

How?

A life

The way in which I miss you chokes my throat
and burns my eyes

If I had known such an ache would have been
created from leaving you

I can't help but wonder what I'll do

If there comes a day when the sun rises without
you

Garden of Scars

May the flowers of your light show through the scars of your darkest night

Let it be proof that the garden of your life is deep-rooted

Because your scars are not weakness but evidence that life shows through

Believe in your light and if you can't, I'll do it for you

And the Soul

I'm not sure you understand how loud the words
in my head scream

In comparison to the soft whispers my heart
loves to dream

Goodbye

The hardest thing isn't always saying goodbye,
but instead knowing when to do so

Because it's easy when it's just a word whispered
into the night

But it's harder when it's screamed from a broken
heart

Because goodbye is too permanent a word for
how dramatically you've changed me